COURAGE AND REDEMPTION

SIX BATTLE PRINCIPLES
FROM THE STORY OF JOSHUA

DUSTIN RIVENBARK

COURAGE AND REDEMPTION
SIX BATTLE PRINCIPLES FROM THE STORY OF JOSHUA

Copyright © 2019 Dustin Rivenbark.

All rights reserved. No part of this book may be used or reproduced by any means, graphic, electronic, or mechanical, including photocopying, recording, taping or by any information storage retrieval system without the written permission of the author except in the case of brief quotations embodied in critical articles and reviews.

iUniverse books may be ordered through booksellers or by contacting:

iUniverse
1663 Liberty Drive
Bloomington, IN 47403
www.iuniverse.com
1-800-Authors (1-800-288-4677)

Because of the dynamic nature of the internet, any web addresses or links contained in this book may have changed since publication and may no longer be valid. The views expressed in this work are solely those of the author and do not necessarily reflect the views of the publisher, and the publisher hereby disclaims any responsibility for them.

Any people depicted in stock imagery provided by Getty Images are models, and such images are being used for illustrative purposes only.
Certain stock imagery © Getty Images.

Scripture quotations marked HCSB are from the Holman Christian Standard Bible®, HCSB®. Copyright ©1999, 2000, 2002, 2003 by Holman Bible Publishers. Used by permission. Holman Christian Standard Bible®, Holman CSB®, and HCSB® are federally registered trademarks of Holman Bible Publishers

ISBN: 978-1-5320-8805-6 (sc)
ISBN: 978-1-5320-8804-9 (e)

Library of Congress Control Number: 2020902070

Print information available on the last page.

iUniverse rev. date: 02/13/2020

For Callie Grace
Rivenbark, Vicki Griffin,
and Nancy Rivenbark

Contents

Acknowledgments ix

1. Afraid to Dream 1
2. Prepare for Battle 13
3. Obtain Spies 25
4. Cross the Jordan 39
5. Defeat the Enemy 51
6. Claim Your Inheritance 65
7. Live Your Legacy 79

My Prayer for You 89

Acknowledgments

I can't even begin to acknowledge all the people who invested time in me or helped me with life lessons that ultimately led to creating this book. This life is such an adventure of ups and downs, and I am so thankful for the people who God has placed in my life.

Thanks to my wife, Aimee, and my children for always supporting me and putting up with my craziness. We have been through so much together. I love you.

Special thanks to Mary Asher (stepmother) and Ed (father) for always picking me up and helping me when I was lost. The two of you have imparted so much love and wisdom onto me that I could never pay back.

Thanks to Nancy (grandmother) and David (grandfather) for never giving up on me and instilling in me the value of hard work. I will love you forever.

Thank you to Uncle Lee for stepping into my messiness at just the right times.

Huge thanks to Ryan Clements, Derek Rumler, and Paul Enfinger for being great men of God and for always supporting me.

Thanks to Reggie Washington for his passion for Jesus and for helping me discover God in such a powerful way.

Huge thanks to all my brothers and sisters—Logan, Emily, Mary Charles, Mallie, Whitt, and Ryn—I hope that you know I love you very much.

Thanks to my church family at Watermark Church. What Jesus did through this church and its members changed my life!

Special thanks to all my brothers offshore. You guys have had such a powerful influence on me. I can never thank you enough.

Heavenly thanks to Vicki (mother). You taught me how to fight! I am so grateful for the lessons you have taught me both directly and indirectly. I love you, Momma.

Chapter 1
Afraid to Dream

"For I know the plans I have for you"—
this is the Lord's declaration—"plans
for your well-being, not for disaster,
to give you a future and a hope."

—*Jeremiah 29:11*

Beep, beep, beep. My head spun as I listened to all the machines beeping and chirping. My mother lay dying on a hospital bed. I was so confused. All these tubes and IVs were running everywhere: through her nose, in her mouth, and sticking into her arm. *I must be going crazy,* I thought. *Is this even real? What is going on?*

At that moment, the doctor walked in. A rather short man, he was dressed really nicely. With his dark complexion and strong accent, he appeared to be of African descent. "Hello," the doctor said as he shook my hand.

"What's the latest, Doctor?" I asked.

"Well, your mother's organs are shutting down. She will not survive through the night. Her body is building up massive amounts of lactic acid, which is why her hands and feet are swelling."

There were, in fact, massive amounts of swelling in her hands and feet.

"What do we do?" my grandmother asked.

"Well, Mrs. Williams, if it were my mother or daughter, I would stop all medicines and let her expire naturally."

"Expire naturally?" I exclaimed.

"Yes, Dustin," he said. "Your mother has had a massive drug overdose. Her body is shutting down. I'm so sorry, but it's the right thing to do in this situation."

Wow! A drug overdose? Is this how it all ends? I left the room and found an empty conference room. I shut the door and fell to my knees. "Father, I need you now more than ever."

At this point, I would love to tell you that a miracle happened, that God healed my mother that day, and that she made a full recovery and turned from her addiction, but that's not what happened. My mother died on that hospital bed. I was hurt, scared, and confused, and this would be one more scar that would deeply wound me.

Just months prior to my mother passing away, my wife and I lost our second daughter, Callie Grace, to Potter syndrome. She had not developed a functioning kidney or bladder; therefore, she would not survive outside the womb.

Callie Grace passed away one month shy of full term. Holding our baby was one of the hardest things my wife and I have ever had to go through.

My mother passing away while I lay across her chest would definitely rank right up there with Callie.

All of this took the wind right out of my sails. I found myself broken, lost, and afraid. Would this be the straw that broke the camel's back for me? Just to add insult to injury, I watched my entire family circle up and spend their last moments with my grandmother as she passed away just months after losing my mother.

Within one year's time, I witnessed death at the beginning of life with my baby, Callie Grace; at the middle of life with my mother; and at the end of life with my grandmother. With all of this being said, I walked away with a valuable lesson. We only get one shot at this life. What are you going to do with it? I really had two choices: fight or flight!

How could I fight through the pain and scars of life? Somewhere deep inside this pain, there was a desire to be free. How could I ever move forward after all of this? I was afraid of dreaming while living in fear of the unknown. My life had been quite unusual, to say the least. The only way to push through the pain and the scars was to find a system that would give me a road map to freedom. Continue on this journey with me as we uncover the six battle principles from the story of Joshua.

ENTER THE UNKNOWN

> After the death of Moses the Lord's servant, the Lord spoke to Joshua son of Nun, Moses's assistant: "Moses my servant is dead. Now you and all the people prepare to cross over the Jordan to the land I am giving the Israelites."
> (Joshua 1:1–2)

Joshua, a valiant warrior and devout follower of Moses, was scared upon hearing the news that his leader was dead. Joshua and the Israelites had followed Moses out of bondage and slavery in Egypt, and they had been wandering in the wilderness for forty years. Right out of the gate, in the story of Joshua, we find Joshua and the Israelites being handed a crushing blow or a crushing start. A fearful warrior was destined to lead. Joshua, an expert warrior, had been trained to overcome adversity. He would unfold one of the best battle plans the world had ever seen.

As I stared at the text, it led me to the title of my book: *Courage and Redemption*. I thought, *Yes! Wow, that's it. This embodies the story of Joshua. Not just the real story but really the untold story. Why? Because Joshua had scars!*

Joshua was the warrior who led the Israelites into the Promised Land. He was mighty, victorious, and larger than life! That's the Joshua we want. The problem is that we don't think about the crushing. The crushing is what I want to drive home here.

Before Joshua was a valiant leader—and before everyone respected and followed him—he was born a slave in Egypt. That would have placed Joshua right in the middle of the torment that the Israelites faced every day. He was raised under the cruel taskmasters of the day.

Joshua experienced the bondage and the horror that Moses was pulling them out of during the Exodus, which is so important. Can you imagine the collapsing weight of growing up in a life of beatings, a life of survival and fear? What kind of psychological toll does this take on someone day in and day out? I can't even imagine the thought of my family members and my closest friends being snatched out of the line right beside me and being tied up and unmercifully beaten in front of my eyes.

Before you understand the purpose of the Creator, you must understand the scars of the process. Joshua endured pain, hurt, fear, sacrifice, and abandonment early in his life; perhaps that is what made Joshua such a strong leader when it was his time. It can be hard to follow a leader who has never been tested.

T. D. Jakes likens this process of hurt and abandonment to that of a baby eaglet. He tells us to think about an eagle. An eagle understands this probably as good as anyone. A baby eaglet knows nothing but good things. He has a beautiful nest and is fed daily. Life is great until his mother comes along and pushes him out of the nest. As the bird is falling, panicking, flapping his wings, and feeling scared and confused, he thinks, *How could my mother do this to me?* Suddenly, the eaglet feels resistance between his wings, and the panic begins to subside. It's not long before the eaglet starts to fly and soar and know what it means to truly be an eagle.

> "For I know the plans I have for you"—this is the Lord's declaration—"plans for your well-being, not for disaster, to give you a future and a hope." (Jeremiah 29:11)

It is so easy to see the disaster surrounding our circumstance, and we can completely miss the hope and the future part. Perhaps God knows this all too well about our finite minds because he tells Joshua three times in the first nine verses to be "strong and courageous." Three times in the first nine verses! This shows us the human characteristics that could cripple Joshua if left unchecked. Fear is a four-letter word with devastating consequences. This four-letter word can bring opportunities to stand up for something or cripple you to the point that it renders you utterly useless.

We must fight through the fear in order to see the opportunities. How do we fight through the fear? How do we fight through the scars?

> This book of instruction must not depart from your mouth; you are to meditate on it day and night so that you may carefully observe everything written in it. For then you will prosper and succeed in whatever you do. (Joshua 1:8)

Listen to me. The only way to stand on the Word of God is to know what the Word of God says. There is no other way. There is life-changing power in the Word of God.

The goal of this book is to give you six key battle principles from the book of Joshua. These principles will change your life, and they will help you to overcome life's obstacles and become the best version of yourself. This strategy was formulated by one of the best warriors to walk the planet: Joshua! Here are the six principles. Ready? Okay, can I get a drumroll? All right, all right, maybe not.

The six key battle principles:

1. Prepare
2. Obtain Spies
3. Cross the Jordan

4. Defeat the Enemy
5. Claim Your Inheritance
6. Live Your Legacy

These six principles will be explained throughout this book. The best way to maximize its potential is to take it slowly, reflect, and take each principle to heart. This book will take you down deep into your biggest hurts or regrets in life, but if each principle is worked out, it will empower you to push through the scars and come out swinging.

BACK TO THE BASICS

Putting this book together was no small feat, but once I committed myself to working out these principles in my own life, God showed up and worked miracles in my life and the lives of my family.

Having lived through my parents' divorce at an early age and being surrounded by difficult circumstances (fighting, drugs, heavy drinking, and feelings of uncertainty about the future), one can imagine my self-esteem issues and lack of confidence. I was always drawn to the roughest crowds because they were the first to show me love and attention. This began a terrible, spiraling-out-of-control lifestyle that lasted into my twenties.

My father had worked offshore on drilling rigs ever since I was a kid. When I found myself desperate to end the lifestyle I had created, I gave him a call. During this call, my father heard the sound of a hungry man. He knew that I was serious and ready to change.

Over the next ten years, I became a hardworking oilfield hand. I was rough and tough to the core and determined to succeed. I felt like I had black oil pumping through my veins.

I was an AB seaman (able-bodied seaman) in the marine department and was trying to make it into the Subsea SWAT team. This team was dedicated to jumping from rig to rig and assisting subsea departments with rig moves. The subsea department was in charge of everything below the surface and the surface equipment that went along with it.

During rig moves, the daily life of a subsea engineer consists of maintenance and upgrades to the rig's BOP (blowout preventer) and surface equipment. The BOP is a sixty-five-foot, eight-hundred-thousand-pound hunk of complex iron. Its job is to latch onto the seafloor by lowering it through the moon pool (a huge rectangular opening in the center of the rig) by seventy-five-foot joints of riser lowered down from the rig floor. It really is amazing to watch.

Once latched, the BOP is equipped with pipe rams and shear rams. Powered by hydraulics, the pipe rams can be used to hang off drill pipe, for testing, or for many other uses. The shear rams do just that ... shear pipe! Blind shear rams have the ability to shear pipe and close off the well in case of a blowout, hence the name blowout preventer.

Engineers and assistants with dirty faces could often be seen hanging off of this eight-hundred-thousand-pound animal in harnesses and carrying huge pipe wrenches. I was training with those guys during my off time (after my twelve-hour day as a seaman), and working for weeks at a time. We worked three weeks offshore, and then we had three weeks off. Needless to say, I was gaining much respect in the subsea world.

I learned so much about chain of command and preparation during these ten years, and it helped me understand and respect the story of Joshua. I don't know if I could have ever truly understood the deep impact of the story without having faced adversity myself. Every day was a battle. Every day was something new. Every day was something exciting. We had to come together to plan and execute because lives depended on it.

After accepting Christ one night in a Bible study, which was held every Wednesday night on my rig, I knew that nothing would ever be the same. After many conversations about my faith with Reggie Washington, the leader of our Bible study, and my first mission trip with my church, I felt called to go into the ministry.

After two years of fighting the call of ministry, the bottom fell out of the oil industry. Two hundred thousand jobs were lost, and mine was one of them. I soon found myself as the youth pastor at Watermark Church in Ashford, Alabama. As I was ready to take on the world and live my fairy-tale ending, the wind was taken right out of my sails.

Numb, shaken, and completely lost after the loss of our daughter, my mother, and my grandmother during my first year in ministry, I was left once again to pick up the pieces. This time, things were different. I wasn't just facing the fear of something happening only to me—like the fighting that took place between my mom and stepdad in my younger years. I was feeling the pressure of a grieving wife, my daughter Brianna was trying to make sense of it all, and my family was trying to navigate the loss of my mother and grandmother. I was lost and completely torn apart. How could we ever put the pieces back together?

I still remember the words my wife said to me at one of my lowest points: "Dustin, we have to get back to the basics." No truer words have ever been spoken. We dove into community and let people help us and lift us up while turning to God's Word for revival.

This is where we find the very first key battle principle from the story of Joshua.

REFLECTION

1. What is the *biggest* obstacle that you are facing right now? What is the smallest?

   _____
   _____
   _____

2. What does God telling Joshua to be "strong and courageous" three times in the first nine verses of chapter 1 tell us about how Joshua may have been feeling?

   _____
   _____
   _____

3. What are the six key battle principles that we can glean from the story of Joshua?

   _____
   _____
   _____

Chapter 2
Prepare for Battle

> Get provisions ready for yourselves, for within three days you will be crossing the Jordan to go in and take possession of the land the Lord your God is giving you to inherit.
>
> —*Joshua 1:11*

Preparation is the first key battle principle that we find. Take notice that Joshua says to get provisions ready for yourself first. At first glance, it sounds a little selfish, doesn't it? Get supplies ready for me first? What is that all about?

Think about a flight attendant giving flight instructions about the oxygen masks at high altitude. What does she say about that oxygen mask? Put your mask on first! That's because you are no good to anyone else if you can't breathe. It's the same concept here. Perhaps you are suffocating. Maybe you are sure that God spoke to you about that certain situation, but you are tired of waiting. Maybe you feel forgotten. Perhaps you are suffocating to the point that you question God's existence at all.

Just say it. Let's be real. Can we be real here? Some of us carry scars. I'm talking about some really big scars. I know because I carry them too. Before we move any further, I want to stand in the gap and apologize.

Some of us need to hear this before we can move forward. I want to apologize for the person who hurt you. The person who didn't give you what you needed. The person who took from you and took from you and never gave back. I'm sorry, son. I'm sorry, daughter. I'm sorry, brother. I'm sorry, sister, mother, father, husband, wife, and friend. I'm so sorry. I didn't know how that would make you feel. I love you.

I hope that hearing these words can begin to help you relax. Maybe it won't. Perhaps it makes the feelings worse. Please pause, go back, and read those words again. Before you can ever heal, you have to feel. You must not hide or shove down your feelings and hurts any longer. Refuse to numb or dumb down your pain. It's okay to not be okay. We just can't stay that way.

For a lot of us, this preparation will take much scripture and counseling. It may take years to overcome a lifetime of abuse. I hear you, and I agree with you, but you have to hear the promise. God said, "I will not leave you or abandon you."

You are not alone. If you are on the move and things are going great, you are not alone. If you are in recovery, you are not alone. If you are fighting in the trenches to find courage and redemption from a lifetime of bad decisions or horrible memories, you are not alone! There is power in the name of Jesus.

We must prepare! I'm not talking about cleaning up before you show up. I'm talking about naming it. I'm talking about taking ownership of it. I'm talking about identifying the hurt. I'm talking about taking a stand. I'm talking about refusing to suffocate any longer.

PRACTICE MAKES PERFECT

"Man overboard!" The words came piercing through the PA system of our eight-hundred-foot drillship. We were stationed on a well in the Gulf of Mexico.

"This is not a drill. I repeat. This is not a drill."

This was immediately followed by the blowing of the ship's whistle and alarms ringing.

When I heard the call, I was walking along "the green mile" (a long stretch of walkway leading from the forecastle to the stern of the ship). I ran up the nearest set of stairs that led up to the FRC (fast rescue craft), skipping every other step.

When I got to the top of the deck, I knew exactly what my job was. As part of the fast rescue team, we had these drills almost weekly. I opened the container with all our life jackets and rescue gear and grabbed my jacket.

The ship's bosun had made it onto the scene—along with my father. It was extremely rare for my father to be on my drilling rig, but he was an offshore surveyor and happened to be doing a survey on our rig. Next on the scene was our rig mechanic. Everything was happening extremely fast, but we had practiced for this situation for years.

A rescue situation required three people: a certified driver of the FRC (our bosun/AB seaman), a mechanic (in case of boat trouble), and a trained deckhand (AB seaman). I was the trained deckhand.

My father jumped in and helped us put on our life jackets and get in the boat. As we entered the boat, we assumed our positions. My bosun went to the helm, the rig mechanic went to the seat located just forward of the engine compartment, and I went to the front of the FRC and held on to the safety straps inside the boat. We unfastened the ratchet straps that held the FRC in place, and we were ready.

The bosun yelled, "Ready?"

We yelled back, "Ready!"

He grabbed the handle to the release cord on the lifeboat davit and pulled.

The boat made a quick jerking motion and then stabilized into a steady descent.

As we got close to the choppy waves—the sun was out, but it was very windy and high seas—we paused for a moment to make sure the engine was good, the steering wheel was turned away from ship (we did not want to get forced into the side of the ship in such strong waves), and I was in place to release us from the davit.

Once everything was a go, we made our final descent. Splash! We hit the water. I quickly lifted the latch, releasing us from the davit cable, and we were off.

The bosun hit the throttle, and I dove back into my position at the front of the boat. As we pulled away from the ship, I stood up on my knees in order to look for the man who had fallen overboard. It wasn't long before I spotted him. "Over there!"

About fifty yards in front of us, I saw a line stretching from the ship to the water. Someone had thrown down a life ring.

"I see it," the bosun said. "Get into position."

I assumed the position, and as we got closer, I saw the life ring swelling up and down the waves and what appeared to be an arm wrapped through it.

As we approached, I was fairly sure that I could pull him into the boat by myself, so I didn't call for the mechanic to come and help. I didn't realize he was a part of the crew that had been brought out to the rig to build scaffolding around the outside of the ship for repairs and upgrades. This meant that, below the surface, he had on a harness, a work vest, a tool belt, and a ten-foot piece of scaffolding attached to his lanyard.

I had trouble grabbing him because he had managed to get one arm and his head through the life ring. On top of that, he seemed to be fighting against me and panicking. I knew I was in trouble. I yelled for the mechanic to give me a hand. I grabbed one side of the man, and he grabbed the other side. I said, "On three, we will catch him on the swell of the waves and drag him in. One. Two. Three!" We dragged him in—and he landed right on top of us.

He burst into tears and said, "Thank you! Thank you! Thank you! I thought I was going to die."

I kept reminding him that he was okay and told him to try to relax.

"Thank you, God," he said. "Thank you for sending them."

As we rolled him over onto the deck, through his torn shirt, I couldn't help but notice some serious bruises and cuts. This man didn't just fall. He was hurt and was lucky to be alive!

We made it back to the ship, latched up to the davit, and began our climb back to the main deck. We were met by the rig medic and the stretcher team who had been observing the whole time. We unhooked all the man's gear and handed him off to the stretcher team. They took him away to the ship's hospital, and I never saw him again. He was sent by helicopter for evaluation. Although we later heard that he was okay, I will never forget the look in his eyes. That man was unsure of his fate in that moment.

The next day, management called for a safety stand-down in the galley to review everything that had happened and to discuss how to prevent it from happening again in the future. I remember all the buzz in the air about the dramatic events that took place the day before. People were patting us on the back in some sort of strange hero's welcome.

Although we were being celebrated for a job well done, I knew why we were so effective. Practice makes perfect! This whole idea of preparation is so important for facing obstacles in life. A term we used the oil field still sticks with me to this day: "If you stay ready, you don't have to get ready."

When challenges come—and they will come—we need to have a system or a set of practices to run these challenges through. The length of time spent in each principle varies and fluctuates, but the principles stay the same. Maybe it was a life-altering event or something devastating or hurtful. Whatever the case, you must get provisions ready for yourself first! Having an arsenal of Bible verses and God-given truths to instill in our hearts is the equivalent of having supplies in our life raft.

Joshua knew he was good at what he did, and he knew the value of preparation. Men must be trained. Food must be stored. Clothes must be packed. Whatever is needed for the journey, it all starts right here in this very first key principle. Prepare!

Prayer is the most powerful weapon that we possess. We often find Joshua waking in the wee hours of the morning to prepare for his day by consulting with God through prayer. Oftentimes, we talk to people in passing and say things like, "I'll be praying for you, brother." We might even be asked to keep someone in our thoughts and prayers, and we say, "Sure." However, we move on with our days without ever actually taking the time to pray for them.

Prayer is the single most effective way to bring clarity into the chaos that can be felt through a trial, a circumstance that seems out of control, or any other situation. I like to say, "Prayer is not the least we can do—it's the most we can do!" We are called into a right relationship with God through the death and resurrection of Jesus Christ. When we pray, God listens.

Joshua knew the importance of God's Word and obeying his commands. When we are unsure where to start with preparation—or we are unsure where to begin in this principle—pray. Pray for God to speak to you and help you see your value and potential. No matter what has happened or how bad it seems, never forget that God created you and desires a relationship with you.

Oftentimes, our preparation comes in the form of counseling. There is nothing wrong with seeing a professional to help you through your scars. I am a firm believer that God put people here to help us and to offer insights that we might miss on our own. It's important to know that the preparation process can last throughout the other key battle principles we will be learning about. It may last throughout all of them. That is okay. You are not weird. You have been deeply wounded, and sometimes this is a lifelong process. While it is important not to skip any steps, you should be aware that several of these steps overlap one another.

One of the hardest things about being broken is the crushing weight that collapses the backbone of your dreams. The one thing that you felt called to do or born for quickly fades to black. It almost becomes a ghostly silhouette that hides in the shadows of your heart.

For Joshua, the preparation process served a great purpose. It prepared his people for the coming challenges and served as a reminder to keep moving even through the loss of his mentor, Moses. Yes, Joshua would have grieved, but from a battlefield mind-set, he knew that the war rages on and there was still work to do. His mind-set and his battle principles gave him purpose in the midst of the pain; therefore, he had direction through the storm.

Think back! Take the time to step back and remember what really fires your engines. What is sitting idle in the background but ready to explode at any moment? Let us dare to dream again. I know you are crushed, hurt, and maybe even terrified, but a fire is burning within you. A state of urgency is fanning the flames. The dark silhouette that has been so lost in the background of your heart is slowly taking shape and beginning to rise.

At this point, you have to make a decision. Do you stop reading, put the book down, walk away, and continue the path of least resistance, which leads to nowhere good, or do you pause, take a deep breath, and allow God to use your scars as a tool to help advance the Gospel. Yes, you heard me right. You can turn this pain, this fear, this scar into a positive weapon to use against the shame and despair it has caused.

It won't be easy, and the road is long, but through Jesus's

power, any pain can be healed—and anything dead can be brought back to life:

> No one will be able to stand against you as long as you live. I will be with you, just as I was with Moses. I will not leave you or abandon you. (Joshua 1:5)

These words began to instill courage and hope in Joshua as he stared at the daunting task of leading the Israelites out of the wilderness and into the Promised Land.

Preparation is the first key battle principle in the story of Joshua because it sets the tone for the entire journey. Fighting through the scars and living out his legacy is the first step to moving forward!

REFLECTION

1. What is one way that you can personally start to put the battle principle of *preparation* into motion?

   _____
   _____
   _____

2. What is meant by practice makes perfect? What are some things we can do to stay ready?

   _____
   _____
   _____

3. What is a dream you used to have that seems to have faded?

   _____
   _____
   _____

Chapter 3
Obtain Spies

> Joshua son of Nun secretly sent two men as spies from the Acacia Grove, saying, "Go and scout the land, especially Jericho." So they left, and they came to the house of a prostitute named Rahab, and stayed there.
>
> —*Joshua 2:1*

The second thing Joshua did was send spies! The second key battle principle is to obtain spies. I'm not talking about the 007 kind of spies. We need *people*. Joshua sent two spies out to scour the land. I think it's really important that Joshua only sent two. This just so happens to be the same number of spies out of the twelve Moses sent into Canaan who came back with a belief that the Israelites could conquer the land (one of them was Joshua).

Do you think Joshua learned a valuable lesson through that trial or situation? The lesson is not necessarily about the quantity of people speaking into your life, but it might be about the quality of people speaking into your life. I can't stress the importance of having positive, life-giving people in your life. You need people who will help you through the various phases of working out these battle principles in your life. One of the biggest mistakes I made early on was adopting the false idea that I didn't need anyone. I thought I could do it by myself. That was completely false. Having a solid support system is the only way to overcome adversity and turn that trial into a weapon for God's glory.

Joshua sent these spies out to scour the land, and that's when we pick up with the story of Rahab (a prostitute who hid the spies from the king's officials). That was a great moment in time and a great story; I encourage all of you to read it. There is so much about how God can literally use anybody at any point in their lives, but I don't want you to miss a truly pivotal moment:

> And (she) said to them, "I know that the Lord has given you this land and that the terror of you has fallen on us, and everyone who lives in the land is panicking because of you." (Joshua 2:9)

Listen to me right now and listen well. The enemy knows the scars that you carry. He knows the burden you are under, but he also knows what you are capable of. He knows that if you get one second to use those scars for the glory of God, there will be a revival in the land. The enemy is panicking. You need people who have been there. You need people who have been to the other side and come back with a message of hope.

The two spies came back to Joshua and said, "The Lord has handed over the entire land to us. Everyone who lives in the land is also panicking because of us" (Joshua 2:24).

Joshua had faith in God, and he surrounded himself with people who had faith in God. Look around your camp. Take inventory of the people that surround you. Do you have people? I'm not talking about bodies; I'm talking about life-giving, truth-holding people. I'm talking about people who don't just tell you what you want to hear. I'm talking about people who tell you what you need to hear in order to draw you closer to your Promised Land, which is your purpose.

PURPOSING THE STORM

A couple of months ago, a friend was fighting for his life in the hospital. I will call him Craig. His battle was cancer. The cancer had caused so many health issues and turned his life upside down. I walked into his hospital room, and he lost it. He started crying, and he told me how he was not ready to die. He was tired of going in and out of hospital rooms. He was tired of being stuck by needles and feeling like a pincushion. And then he dropped the bomb: He said, "My life is no longer valuable. It feels like I'm in prison, and I will never get out." Craig had been informed that he didn't have long to live.

I could not relate to his feelings about cancer, but I could certainly relate to him feeling like he was in prison. That is where this second key battle principle is *vital*. There are several ways that someone could react to hearing this kind of response from a friend, but I knew I needed to show him purpose. He needed to know that—even as confusing as it sounds—we can find purpose in the storm.

As I looked at him, I prayed for the right words to say. I said, "Craig, some of the most powerful drug cartels are run from inside prisons." I certainly don't condone that lifestyle, but I needed him to understand my point. I said, "No matter the circumstance, no matter the hurt, we can use this for the glory of God. We can turn this into a weapon to smash the enemy's head."

Do you see what I did there? Two things occurred. I gave him purpose in the storm, and I went from "he" to "we." I let him know that he wasn't alone. There were people fighting in the trenches right alongside him.

"Craig?" I said.

"Yes, Dustin," he replied.

"How much you trust in God and represent our powerful Creator will speak volumes to your family and to each and every person you come in contact with here at this hospital."

After a great life-giving talk and prayer time, he finally started to come to the realization that he could be a leader for his family and for others from right there in his hospital bed.

That was the last conversation I had with my friend, but you can rest assured that I walked into a hopeless situation and put a big smile on a friend's face. This shows the power of having life-giving people in your life. No matter what is going on around you or inside you, you can still have purpose.

THE POWER OF THE PURGE

The Israelites and Joshua would have known that Moses's passing was a devastating blow to everything they knew at that point. However, by preparing and allowing the right people to speak into Joshua's life, he was able to see through the fog of grief and into the purpose of God. His purpose was bringing his people into the Promised Land and acquiring all that God had in store for them.

You might not see it now, but there is life on the other side of fear. There is life on the other side of my scars. Had Joshua placed the wrong people of influence over him, there is no way we would even be talking about him today. There is power in speaking life into others.

Take inventory of the people who surround your camp. Take inventory of the biggest influencers speaking to you right now. Don't be afraid. Do it now! Put this book down and ponder the words that you have been given over the past few years. Do they match up with what God says about you? Do the words bring life or death? Do they bring you up or down?

The power of the purge comes from the realization that some people don't deserve to carry the kind of weight over you that you are allowing them to carry. The power of the purge allows you to feel some type of control even when everything else feels out of control. Can it be scary? Yes! Will it be easy? No! Removing people from your circle can be one of the most freeing things you will ever experience, but it can also be one of the hardest things that you will ever do in this life.

This is one of the most urgent priorities to establishing the second key battle principle (obtaining spies). It is of utmost importance to remove all negative spheres of influence before surrounding yourself with the right people to help you move forward.

Removing people or negative influences can be one of the hardest things to do in life. It can cause fear, anxiety, or even pain initially, but remember these powerful words from the Bible:

> Haven't I commanded you: be strong and courageous? Do not be afraid or discouraged, for the Lord your God is with you wherever you go. (Joshua 1:9)

Joshua had a great mentor in Moses. Moses persevered through all the negativity of people complaining and wanting to go back to Egypt when things got tough in the wilderness. He knew the importance of looking ahead and not giving in to all the fears that tend to rise up when you enter the unknown. Through a strong relationship with God and a passion for his people, Moses would surround himself with people who would help him advance the kingdom.

Try to imagine what would have happened if Joshua had collapsed under the weight of the loss of Moses and caved to the cries of the people who wanted to go back to Egypt. That wouldn't have just altered the story; it would have altered history. God is in control, but we still have important roles to play in the kingdom of God.

NOW I HAVE NO ONE

Sometimes the purge leaves us with a feeling of loneliness. It appears to push us back down into the hurt that has plagued us for so long. At this point, you can hear these words echoing through eternity: "Great, Dustin. Now I have no one." For some of us, the idea of being lonely keeps us in harmful relationships and situations for far too long.

Being in the Word of God plays a major role in your psyche:

> Do not fear, for I am with you; do not be afraid, for I am your God. I will strengthen you; I will help you; I will hold onto you with My righteous right hand. (Isaiah 41:10)

You must get to the point where you are able to embrace the loneliness. You need the freedom to begin the first steps in working out the six key battle principles in your life.

What is that dream again? I can almost hear it whispering, "You can do this." Quit fighting against the generational curse of slavery to an addiction. Quit fighting against the hurt or pain you have endured. Quit fighting the vivid memory of that tragic day. You must believe the words of Matthew when Jesus stated, "With God, all things are possible" (Matthew 19:26).

It's time to face the guilt or the shame that you have been chained to for all this time. Realize that Christ died on that cruel, rugged cross and rose again three days later with our freedom in his hands. If you put your trust and belief in Christ and Christ alone, you have been set free. It's not Christ and your emotions. It's not Christ and your addictions. It's not Christ and your abusive relationship. It's Christ who sets me free. Face the darkest fear in your mind, tell it that the chains are gone, and say, "Because of Christ, I am free."

Freedom is found in community, and I'm not just saying that because I am in ministry. If you are in a place of uncertainty right now—if you are fearful, lonely, or depressed—get to a church! Please don't wait. I know the stereotypes that you may have heard about your local church. I get it, but please know that they aren't all like that. It wasn't until I found community in the body of Christ (the local church) that I was able to break the chains of loneliness in my brokenness. We must have "spies." We must have people watching out for our well-being. God created us to be relational beings. You can do this. Fight the urge to remain in the comfort of what's known and move forward into the beauty of life and what God has in store for your future.

TOO MESSY

When I found myself at my absolute lowest, I realized that I could not pull myself out. I didn't even know where to begin. I was one year into my ministry, and my life had completely fallen apart. I was tired. I had absolutely no clue what tomorrow would bring, but I felt certain it wouldn't bring anything good. Life was too messy.

It wasn't until my wife and I decided to get back to the basics that we realized there was hope. The mess in and of itself was a gift from God, and it allowed us to use the great challenges that God was helping us overcome. Wow, a gift? Can this pain really be a gift?

> And not only that, but we also rejoice in our afflictions, because we know that affliction produces endurance, endurance produces proven character, and proven character produces hope. (Romans 5:3–4)

God's Word tells us to "rejoice in our afflictions." What? How is this possible? How do we get from the point of total hurt and grief to that of rejoicing and praise? The answer lies in the last word of the fourth verse: hope! It is through hope that we rejoice. Hope is a future-based word that allows us to see through the fog in order to dream of the future. Hope is a four-letter word that carries great power. Sometimes it is the only thing that keeps us holding on.

In *Cast Away,* Tom Hanks was in a plane crash and left on a desert island for several years. I can't help but think about how lonely and devastating that would have been. How was he able to survive for that long? The answer is hope—and Wilson helped too. Hope is the one pillar or stable structure that is holding up an otherwise collapsing house. Without hope, everything crashes down—and we are left with the pieces.

As long as we have hope, we still have a chance. By rejoicing in our sufferings, we are relinquishing control of our situation to God. By surrounding yourself with positive people, you are leaving a glimmer of hope in an otherwise dark room. Maybe some of the pieces that don't seem to fit when you try to put them back together are due to the company that you keep. Perhaps the people surrounding you are not strong enough to help you lift the sheer weight of the pieces. The pain is too heavy. Some influences that we allow into our lives are too weak spiritually. They may not have the spiritual strength to offer the kind of help you need.

A great example of this in ministry is the different funerals we attend. There is always a big difference in the tone of funerals between families with no hope and families with hope. The families who are confident that their loved ones are resting in the arms of Jesus have so much more life and joy in their spirits than the families who consider death as something final. That's it? There is no more to life? How depressing it must be to not have any future hope of anything greater.

When life gets too messy, we must surround ourselves with people who have been through the fire and come back bearing messages of hope. These people give us strength and that extra push when we feel as though we can't go on.

REFLECTION

1. What does it mean to obtain spies? Why are they important?
   _____
   _____
   _____

2. How can you rejoice in your afflictions?
   _____
   _____
   _____

3. What must you do when life gets too messy?
   _____
   _____
   _____

Chapter 4
Cross the Jordan

Therefore, since we also have such a large cloud of witnesses surrounding us, let us lay aside every hindrance and the sin that so easily ensnares us. Let us run with endurance the race that lies before us, keeping our eyes on Jesus, the source and perfecter of our faith. For the joy that lay before him, he endured the cross, despising the shame, and sat down at the right hand of the throne of God.

—Hebrews 12:1

Joshua told the people, "Consecrate yourselves, because the Lord will do wonders among you tomorrow." Then he said to the priests, "Carry the ark of the covenant and go on ahead of the people." So they carried the ark of the covenant and went ahead of them. The Lord spoke to Joshua: "Today I will begin to exalt you in the sight of all Israel, so they will know that I will be with you just as I was with Moses. Command the priests carrying the Ark of the Covenant: When you reach the edge of the water, stand in the Jordan" (Joshua 3:5–8).

Joshua knew crossing the Jordan River was the only way to get to the Promised Land. The only way to get to his destiny was to *move*. He had already prepared. He had already sent spies and been encouraged and empowered to move forward. Now he had to do something. The third key battle principle for Joshua was crossing the Jordan.

The only way to move ahead and acquire all that God has in store for you is to walk straight through the fear. You must prepare. You must obtain spies (people looking out for you), but sooner or later, you have to cross the Jordan. Whatever that obstacle is that you are facing, it's time to act.

Some of you might not be out of the first battle principle yet, and that's okay. You can overlap some of these steps, but you cannot skip them. Remember to take it slowly. Write these principles down as reminders of where you are in your journey. The beauty of the written reminders is being able to see progress. Seeing yourself slowly moving from one principle to the next helps you gain momentum. Gaining traction is a fantastic rearview mirror for seeing how far God has brought you.

In this Christian life, you are either an overcomer or you're overcome. You are either a victor or a victim. It all boils down to whether we are willing to cross the Jordan. I can play the victim here and blame Daddy or blame Momma for my scars.

And, yes, I know they hurt. There is no denying that the *only* way to freedom is to cross the Jordan.

In Deuteronomy, Moses said, "God is bringing us out … so that He may bring us in." Where is God calling you out of? Naming it will help you prepare. Let's start the process. There is definitely a plan for your life, but the only way to victory is going straight through the fear. Is it going to hurt? Yes! Will there be tears? Certainly, but in order to heal, you have to feel.

Once you have people around you, once you are surrounded with a hedge of protection, once you are drenched in God's Word and his love for you, take a step. Take it slowly. I'm right here with you.

I'm reaching back into that dark place where I once was to help you through this journey. There you go! You've got this! Take a step. Take one more step. There it is. Baby steps are fine—in fact, I recommend them.

Martin Luther King Jr. said, "If you can't fly then run, if you can't run then walk, if you can't walk then crawl, but whatever you do you have to keep moving forward."

GOD'S STRENGTH IN THE DEEP

> The priests carrying the ark of the Lord's covenant stood firmly on dry ground in the middle of the Jordan, while all Israel crossed on dry ground until the entire nation had finished crossing the Jordan. (Joshua 3:17)

Picture how the priests carried the ark of the covenant and stood in the Jordan River as a wall of water began to form on one side of the river (cutting off the flow of water that flows into the Dead Sea). They stood there until the entire nation of

Israel had crossed over onto dry ground. Wow—talk about the power of God.

There is so much comfort to be found in this one passage, but I don't want you to miss something that often gets overlooked. Notice that the "wall of water" completely cut off the water from flowing into the Dead Sea. If you know anything about the Dead Sea, then you know that nothing can live in it due to its high salt content. It's really salty! Guess what? Many of us are salty as well. We are tired. We are angry. We are frustrated and unable to free our minds. Nothing good can live there because the salt level is too high.

This is a beautiful symbol of God's ability to change our perspectives and change our hearts. The priests stood firm until the entire nation had finished crossing the Jordan. Will you allow God to radically change your way of thought about who he created you to be? Will you allow the Holy Spirit to stand firm in the river that is allowing you to spend all your energy draining into the Dead Sea? Every time you try to cross it, it sucks you back down again and again and again. Not anymore!

This time is different. This time, you have a strategic plan. This time, you are armed with the truth about who you are and whose you are. You are armed with spies, and those people will not let you drown. Today is different. Feel the atmosphere changing and the temperature shifting within your spirit. Allow yourself to believe again and dream again.

In so many ways, your life can feel like the beginning chapters of an underdog story. I love a good underdog story. The movie *Rudy* is a good example. Rudy was a young man who grew up in a household that was in love with Notre Dame football. They never missed a game. Rudy had a lot of heart but not a lot of brawn—if you know what I mean. He dreamed of playing college football at the University of Notre Dame and entered the team as a walk-on while attending the university. Rudy always showed heart. He never quit, and he never gave up during practice. He was knocked down, but he got back up. He was beaten, and you had to beat him again. He was made fun of, but he didn't care. He was a fighter.

Rudy finally got the chance to dress for the final game of the season, and he didn't play the entire game—until the last play. By then, through the ridicule, through the pain and scars of the game, he had won the respect of the campus. The entire stadium started chanting Rudy's name, and he got to go in for one play. Rudy didn't go down in history as a mega football star, but he did reach his dream through hard work and a warrior attitude. The best thing about all of this is *Rudy* is based on a true story.

You may be thinking, *Yeah, that's nice and all, but my life is stuck in the getting-beaten-down phase of the underdog story.*

In the middle of the trial, in the middle of the storm, take your cue from Joshua 1:8:

> This book of instruction must not depart from your mouth; you are to meditate on it day and night so that you may carefully observe everything written in it. For then you will prosper and succeed in whatever you do.

These were the words that kept Joshua focused and disciplined. In moments of uncertainty, shame, hurt, or fear, he could meditate on God's Word and know there was hope and direction when he needed them most.

Always remember that the size of the storm gives way for God to do exceedingly and abundantly more in and through your hardship. If you feel as though you are the only one who has ever experienced this type of trauma or hurt, remember the words of Ecclesiastes: "There is nothing new under the sun."

There is nothing new—and nothing at all for that matter—that can take God by surprise. God wasn't thrown off or caught off guard by your hurt. God is still in control, which should bring us much comfort.

In the midst of the storm, in the midst of the deep, it is hard to believe in the word *comfort*. How could I ever love again after such a terrible divorce? How could I raise my young daughter after the loss of my wife? How could I possibly provide for my family after the loss of my livelihood and career? These types of questions pierce your heart in the midst of tragedy. Never forget God's strength in the deep.

MAKING THE TRANSITION

When you are crossing your Jordan, it is important to realize that I'm talking about heading toward your purpose. Notice that I didn't just say that you found your purpose. No, in this journey, I want to help you lay down some tracks to run on. If you can find purpose and direction, then you have won half the battle already. When we are in that season of life that God has placed us in, we are heading toward our purpose.

There are seasons of life that we place ourselves in—through dumb decisions or pride—and then there are seasons that God has placed us in. In *those* seasons, we are walking in our calling—or at least heading toward it.

By calling, I mean your purpose. This hit me as a revelation, and I believe God spoke to me, which is the best definition of a calling that I have ever heard. Our calling is where God has placed us for impact—and we are thankful through obedience. This will save you a lot of unnecessary searching and nonfulfillment. This takes so much pressure off you to keep trying to force life to happen.

Where does God have you right now that you can use your scars and your story to make an impact? How can you use your life lessons to improve your situation or the people around you? You are not alone in figuring this out. I am laying the groundwork for you to follow, and you are doing great.

Through the preparation process and obtaining people with your best interests at heart (your spies), you can finally move toward crossing your Jordan. Your Jordan is that powerful inanimate object that is standing in the way of your purpose. Just like Joshua and the Israelites, you have access to the most powerful being in all eternity. God is calling out to you to keep moving. He will be with you every step of the way. Keep going!

Anytime a transition is taking place, it can be scary. My hardest transition was changing my thinking from a victim mind-set to that of being determined to use my scars to help people see the hope on the other side of their pain. At that point, I had so many feelings swelling up inside me. I felt inadequacy and fear. Who was I to have something to offer someone else? What could I say or do that could possibly be of significance to anyone?

Right then, a moment of clarity was spoken over me by my *battle buddy*. My battle buddies are my spies, and they are my accountability partners when I need them. These are the people whom I let speak into my life. I used to let just anyone and everyone have influence in my life if they would speak what I *wanted* to hear, but through the discovery of the second key battle principle, I uncovered how that had to change.

By serving in my local church, putting myself out there, and showing a need for men of faith in my life, I now have true friends who want me to succeed in life. I now have people who add value to my life. I have a group that has my back and is ready for spiritual warfare!

Ryan Clements, my friend and battle buddy, told me that people needed to hear my story. That's it! That was the turning point for me. Right then and right there—through the love and support of someone who I knew had my back—I was empowered to do the impossible. It was not super-fancy theology or a mind-blowing revelation; it was just the truth from a loving friend. I was going to cross my Jordan River. Yes, I had taken a massive blow to my life. I had lost my ten-year career, my daughter, my mother, and my grandmother in a little over a year, but I would not lose the chance to share it with the world. I was going to overcome this devastating trial, and God was going to help me get there.

I immediately turned to life-giving people, and I jumped into the Word of God. I asked God to give me the courage and wisdom to share my testimony and help other people overcome the traumatic events in their lives. I found myself preaching about God's love and grace in jails, in schools, in small groups, and at church and local events. God started using me in powerful ways, and I began to see purpose in the storm. I was moving toward my purpose. I was transitioning across my Jordan, and God was standing firm in the deep.

I'd love to tell you that all of this was really easy for me, but unfortunately, it wasn't. Just like Joshua was *seeking courage and redemption*, so was I. I was scarred from the storms of life and was seeking courage and redemption from a broken spirit, but God placed the Lion of Judah inside my heart! Jesus would walk with me through the Jordan, through the fear, every step of the way.

Though Joshua carried scars, he learned the value of them—and he learned his purpose through them. He was a warrior. He was a worshipper and a leader. All of this was due to the incredible battles that God was able to lead him through. Joshua had incredible skills as a leader and left us with an amazing battle plan, but what truly sets Joshua apart was his prayerful mind-set. He knew that "with God, all things were possible" (Matthew 19:26).

REFLECTION

1. How was Joshua encouraged and empowered to move forward across the Jordan?

   _____

   _____

   _____

2. Where has God placed you right now so that you can show thankfulness through obedience?

   _____

   _____

   _____

3. What Jordan River is standing in your way?

   _____

   _____

Chapter 5
Defeat the Enemy

You are from God, little children, and you have conquered them, because the one who is in you is greater than the one who is in the world.

—1 John 4:4

Joshua was commissioned to do three things:

- lead Israel into the Promised Land
- defeat the enemy
- claim the inheritance

Now that you are crossing over your Jordan and moving into the Promised Land, you must know that you *will* face opposition. You have an enemy (the devil) that does not want you to succeed: "A thief comes only to steal and kill and destroy. I have come so that they may have life and have it in abundance" (John 10:10).

Joshua was a warrior, and many people associate him as a Christlike figure in the Old Testament. We often associate the crossing of the Jordan River with what happened at Calvary. We associate this with a beautiful picture of us dying to sin and finding redemption through the death and resurrection of Jesus Christ.

THE LORD IS MY BANNER

Jesus was confirmed or commissioned to the people at his baptism in which the Holy Spirit fell on him like a dove. God said, "This is my Son in whom I'm well pleased."

The Amalekites attacked the Israelites, and through obedience, Joshua triumphed:

> The Lord then said to Moses, "Write this down on a scroll as a reminder and recite it to Joshua: I will completely blot out the memory of Amalek under heaven." (Exodus 17:14)

The Lord was commissioning Joshua for a great work in

the future. After this, Moses built an altar and said, "The Lord is my Banner." Wow. This is the type of person I want to be around. Their faith was incredible. Their faith is supernatural.

Joshua is often depicted as a Christlike being, but he wasn't Christ. He was fully man. He was a warrior with weather-beaten eyes who carried really big scars. Once he made it to the Promised Land, he had some battles ahead. He faced opposition. As a warrior, he knew this. The first battle principle told us that he was *prepared*.

Once Joshua got to the Promised Land, he set up memorial stones and circumcised all the Israelites. I'm not giving you any ideas, right? Don't go making a knife out of flint rock and go cutting on, well, anything. No! The point is that he dedicated himself, his people, and his family to the work of the Lord.

In addition to being a warrior, Joshua was a worshipper. Many people believe Joshua was a Christophany or the Lord himself showing up in the Old Testament:

> Then Joshua bowed with his face to the ground in worship and asked him, "What does my lord want to say to his servant?"
>
> The commander of the Lord's army said to Joshua, "Remove the sandals from your feet, for the place where you are standing is holy." And Joshua did that. (Joshua 5:14b–15)

How many of us approach the throne of God in such a way as this before we face a battle or any other situation? Joshua, Moses, and Noah all show us what it means to stand in awe and in reverence of almighty God.

For ten years, I worked on drilling rigs with three weeks on and three weeks off. The time away from home was tough, but life was comfortable. I was climbing to success. I bought land

and sold my house, which we had been trying to sell for two years. We had been trying to get pregnant for four years—and then we got pregnant! God is so good.

Unfortunately, the industry took a downturn and two hundred thousand jobs were lost. Mine was one of them. I had twenty-five acres, a pregnant wife, and no job! I was facing a battle. It felt like I was facing a storm. It was the perfect storm—the type of storm that you pack up all your things and run far away from. However, the problem was that the storm had crept up on me so fast that I couldn't run. I had to stand firm or be destroyed like hurricane debris. Storms come to try our foundations. In those moments, Joshua 1:9 can be a weapon in our arsenal:

> Haven't I commanded you: be strong and courageous? Do not be afraid or discouraged, for the Lord your God is with you wherever you go. (Joshua 1:9)

This has become a staple in my life. In fact, I have it as a decal (like memorial stones) on the wall beside my bed. It's the last thing I see when I go to bed at night and the first thing I see when I wake up.

> The Lord said to Joshua, "Look, I have handed Jericho, its king, and its best soldiers over to you. March around the city with all the men of war, circling the city one time. Do this for six days. Have seven priests carry seven ram's-horn trumpets in front of the ark. But on the seventh day, march around the city seven times, while the priests blow the trumpets." (Joshua 6:2–4)

First, he heard the promise—and then he acted. This is very important to understand in your quest against the enemy. My humanness tells me to react first. My first reaction to losing my job was to immediately run out and get another good-paying job out of sheer panic, and that's what I did. I went out and grabbed a manager's spot at a very demanding job that completely took me away from the church.

Listen to me, folks. If you are being taken away from the church, then you are losing your connection to the body of Christ—end of story! We need each other in order to fulfill the Great Commission. After he hears the promise, he follows the process. Even when the process doesn't make sense, follow it! It is through the process that we defeat the enemy.

> Consider it a great joy, my brothers and sisters, whenever you experience various trials, because you know that the testing of your faith produces endurance. (James 1:2–3)

Endurance wins the race; endurance wins the fight!

> This book of instruction must not depart from your mouth; you are to meditate on it day and night so that you may carefully observe everything written in it. For then you will prosper and succeed in whatever you do. (Joshua 1:8)

We must stay rooted in the Word of God in order to stand firm through the storm.

This life calls for faith. The Bible tells us that faith is the belief in the things unseen, but what if it's more than just believing in spite of evidence? What if it's also obeying in spite of consequence.

Through my human encounter with my circumstance, I received my scars. I misinterpreted my scars as consequence, but they were really a catapult that pushed me forward in my faith. I hope you are getting this.

Joshua and his people circled the city of Jericho for seven days. Even when it didn't make sense, they followed the process. Through faith and obedience—and in spite of the consequences—the Israelites took Jericho.

Everyone wants to preach about Jericho. Yeah, Jericho! Defeat the enemy, hoorah! The Bible says that the Lord was "with Joshua and his fame spread throughout the land." Everyone likes that story, but no one ever talks about the loss right after that:

> The Israelites, however, were unfaithful regarding the things set apart for destruction. Achan son of Carmi, son of Zabdi, son of Zerah, of the tribe of Judah, took some of what was set apart, and the Lord's anger burned against the Israelites. (Joshua 7:1)

The Lord ordered the destruction of everything at Jericho, but a couple of people saw something shiny during the battle. They saw something that was maybe even a little familiar. Even though it wasn't meant for them—and even though it wasn't part of their great promised inheritance—they took it.

How many times during the heat, during the fire, do you look for something familiar or something shiny to elevate your status when you feel lowly? It might be women or men. It could be alcohol or drugs. Hmm ... watch out, Instagram. Watch out, Twitter. Here I come, right?

Yes, but something else has occurred here as well. Through all of the winning and all of the elevating, Joshua doesn't pray first. He seems to go on his own accord.

> Joshua sent men from Jericho to Ai, which is near Beth-aven, east of Bethel, and told them, "Go up and scout the land." So the men went up and scouted Ai. After returning to Joshua they reported to him, "Don't send all the people, but send about two thousand or three thousand men to attack Ai. Since the people of Ai are so few, don't wear out all our people there." So about three thousand men went up there, but they fled from the men of Ai. The men of Ai struck down about thirty-six of them and chased them from outside the city gate to the quarries, striking them down on the descent. As a result, the people lost heart. (Joshua 7:2–5)

I forgot that God was in control, and I acted in my own accord with my new job situation. When I ran out and found this job on my own accord, it left me in a spiritual deficit, which is right where the enemy wants me. He wants me there because he is afraid of my scar. He is afraid that I will seek courage and redemption. He uses those scars as misinterpretations of consequence in the hope that I will fall back instead of seeing my scar as something I am *stronger than*.

Joshua lost the battle. He lost the battle! The famous, mighty warrior lost the battle. Joshua had to do some hard things, and he had to face the problem. He had to approach the disobedient part of the body and deal with it.

Our culture today says, "No! Don't do that. Just leave. Go somewhere else. That's too hard!" If I'm angry at the church or the pastor, I just leave. If I am angry with him or her, I just leave. Instead of doing hard things and dealing with the issues, we leave. We will realize later that we have carried the root of the problem with us. The Lord said to Joshua, "Do not be afraid or discouraged. Take all the troops with you and go attack Ai. Look, I have handed over to you the king of Ai, his people, city, and land" (Joshua 8:1).

God was telling Joshua to go back to the place where he had failed. Shaking off the dust and trying again is one of the hardest things to do in life. What do we mean by "try again"? We just got our butts kicked. However, this time, it was different. This time, they had the promise of God. Israel was victorious against Ai. Through that prayerful mind-set, Joshua and the people conquered Ai.

This was teaching Joshua a valuable lesson. In my life, more often than not, it is up to me. I'm alone in the fight. The weight is on my back, and it is my job to dig myself out. In this hole, I am digging and clawing. I give up, I fold, and I spend the rest of my life in an invisible prison.

Joshua and the Israelites joined forces with others, and when the wicked kings heard about how big they were, they decided to join forces and fight them. In this epic, amazing battle, they were slaughtering one another—and God sent down a hailstorm to fight for Israel.

> So Joshua caught them by surprise, after marching all night from Gilgal. The Lord threw them into confusion before Israel. He defeated them in a great slaughter at Gibeon, chased them through the ascent of Beth-horon, and struck them down as far as Azekah and Makkedah. As they fled before Israel, the Lord

> threw large hailstones on them from the sky along the descent of Beth-horon all the way to Azekah, and they died. More of them died from the hail than the Israelites killed with the sword. (Joshua 10:9–11)

Oh, this is awesome! No movie has anything on this. Israel finally captures the wicked kings, and we figure out the lesson Joshua has learned.

> "Come here and put your feet on the necks of these kings." So the commanders came forward and put their feet on their necks. Joshua said to them, "Do not be afraid or discouraged. Be strong and courageous, for the Lord will do this to all the enemies you fight." (Joshua 10:24b–25)

It's not me. It's not me who fights; it is the God inside me. Oh, y'all! Right in the storm, right through the scars, looking right through the pain, I can praise God.

> No one will be able to stand against you as long as you live. I will be with you, just as I was with Moses. I will not leave you or abandon you. (Joshua 1:5)

No one!

> Neither death nor life, nor angels nor rulers, nor things present nor things to come, nor powers nor height nor depth, nor any other created thing will be able to separate us from the love of

God that is in Christ Jesus our Lord. (Romans 8:38–39)

The enemy might be big and scary—and the obstacle might be daunting and fierce—but there is no other name or being in all eternity that can stand toe to toe with our Lord and Savior. The victory has already been won, and the Bible says that the enemy fell like lightning. Hallelujah!

REFLECTION

1. What three things was Joshua commissioned to do?
   _____
   _____
   _____

2. Why did Joshua and the Israelites suffer the loss at Ai immediately following the victory at Jericho?
   _____
   _____
   _____

3. What distractions can stand in the way of your victory over your obstacles?
   _____
   _____
   _____

Chapter 6
Claim Your Inheritance

In Him we were also made His inheritance, predestined according to the purpose of the One who works out everything in agreement with the decision of His will.

—*Ephesians 1:11*

The fifth key battle principle from the story of Joshua is to claim your inheritance. After the major loss at Ai, Joshua learned a great lesson that taught him to reestablish the prayerful mindset that empowered him from the very beginning. The Lord told Joshua what to do next:

> Do not be afraid or discouraged. Take all the troops with you and go attack Ai. Look, I have handed over to you the king of Ai, his people, city, and land. (Joshua 8:1)

There it is. He now has the promise of God to go back, defeat the enemy, and claim the inheritance. By inheritance, I don't mean a handout. We can look back through the scars and see that nothing came easy, but by inheritance, I mean all that God has for us.

In that stressful job situation, I suddenly remembered the promise of God. I had never walked out of a job before, but I did that day. (I don't recommend this.) Through a powerful prayer session, I started to see it all coming together like a beautiful puzzle. The enemy wanted me down. He wanted me scarred, but by seeking courage and redemption, it was all coming together.

I had always been good with my money, and my land was paid for. That took some of the burden off a loss of salary. I could now go back to church for the body of Christ and the church to lift me up. I could be home with my wife as we both went through a traumatic time during the passing of our daughter. And what the enemy forgot before he tried to scar me was that my pastor and I had been talking about me leaving the oilfield and going into ministry for a year before I finally came home. So what he meant to use for destruction, God used for conformation.

From the very beginning, God's Word says, "You planned evil against me; God planned it for good to bring about the present result—the survival of many people" (Genesis 50:20).

Though the enemy roams the earth like a roaring lion, it is much like a snake with its head cut off. Is it still dangerous? Yes, but its time is limited.

GOD IS FOR YOU

> What, then, shall we say in response to these things? If God is for us, who can be against us? (Romans 8:31)

If God is for us, who can be against us? Wow, what a great verse. No matter where you are in life, you might be on the cusp of something great. Maybe everything is going the way you feel it should go right now. Maybe it is not. Maybe you feel like you are absolutely drowning or like you can never catch a break. No matter what season of life you are in, this verse is powerful. This verse is motivation. You must know that God is for you. And if God is for you, then who could be against you?

But you long to find your true self. Inside, you battle a deep call from your origin, from your creation. You scream intelligent design, and your universe screams intelligent design, but somewhere along the way, you have lost your connection to the Designer.

And it hurts. It really hurts! You are hardwired to believe in something. You are hardwired to worship something. You fill that void and you stuff that void with addictions. You stuff that pain with depression, anxieties, or reality TV. Your heart yearns for what the universe knows is true. You have a purpose.

You have an inheritance to receive. You were created to have a relationship with God. He is relational.

By observing these six key battle principles from Joshua, this particular truth is so clear. God wants to lead you to the Promised Land. He has placed you here for impact, and you are thankful through obedience. In and through the process, in and through the scars, in and through the journey, you can claim your inheritance. You can obtain and live out God's promises.

I love to watch the growth of Joshua throughout his conquests and adventures. We get to see these hard lessons playing out in front of our very eyes. Thankfully, some of these lessons are from a bird's-eye view, but these principles transcend time. All these principles can be used at any stage in any age of life. We find Joshua well advanced in years, still serving, still prayerful, and now able to pass along all he has acquired and gained.

> Joshua was now old, advanced in age, and the Lord said to him, "You have become old, advanced in age, but a great deal of the land remains to be possessed." (Joshua 13:1)

In the next several chapters, Joshua divides the conquered lands according to their designated clans. Right here, we can see the wisdom, strength, and loyalty that have been given to Joshua. He is highly respected and trusted with what has been given to him. Joshua had modeled strength—even when he was weak. He modeled courage—even when he was scared. Now it's time to pass it on.

So much truth is ringing loudly in my brain as I am writing this. There is so much healing to be found in these six key battle principles. Through preparing, obtaining spies, crossing the Jordan, defeating the enemy, and claiming our God-given promises through the claiming of our inheritance, you can finally give back!

This has been a hard yet amazing journey up to this point. We still have one more key battle principle to go, but this is where the pieces start to come together. We can almost see the light at the end of the tunnel. All the pain and hurt can start to be turned into a tool that I can use for good. It can be used for God.

Looking back through the trials and battles that have been won and lost, I can see God's footprints in the sand. Through God's grace and mercy, I am able to use this as a weapon against the enemy. I now get to pass on these key battle principles to you in the same way that Joshua passed on his inheritance.

PERSPECTIVE

We want to *settle* in this life, but we can't. That's why we are always searching. We have the wrong priorities. Philippians 4:13 says, "I can do all things through Christ who strengthens me."

There it is! It's Christ. It's not me—it's Christ! If you can do all things, then that means nothing is impossible. Your perspective is right. Your priorities are right. Christ is the only one who can fill you in the first place. When you seek Christ, you never settle because you are settled! The war against pride is defeated through Christ. God is not a vending machine; you can't just decide that you want something and then pump a few prayers (quarters) into him and have him spit out your desires (snacks). God is relational.

Stop! Think about this now. God of the heavens and the earth, God of the storm, God of the past, present, and future, the Alpha and the Omega is *relational*. God desires a relationship with you. Wow!

I don't know about you, but this puts me on my face! Are you willing to get on your face? Even if you are the CEO of a Fortune 500 company, you need to be small enough to get on your face.

You have to make a choice. Jesus's last command was to "go therefore and make disciples of all nations." In other words, his last command was a call to action. He calls us to action. When Jesus is ready to perform a miracle, there is typically a call to action. Think about the lame man. He said, "Take up your mat and go." This was a call to action.

Perhaps the disciples knew this best. When Peter and the disciples were in the boat, a storm blew up, and they saw Jesus walking on the water. Peter said, "Lord, if it is really you, tell me to come to you." Jesus told him to come. This was a call to action.

When God got ready to create humankind, he breathed his breath. The very essence of that breath was a call to action. God's first command was an action to life.

If Jesus came for us to have abundant life, which is what the Word of God says, then it is settled. It is going to work out. It will be okay. At the end of the day, God is still on the throne and working on my behalf.

Stop pushing! Stop fighting! It's time to let go and let God. Whatever that means for you. Whether it's your job, your finances, or your kids, take it to God. He cares for you. In a fallen world, it's almost natural for us to store up our treasures in barns, bank accounts, 401(k)s, and other false securities. It's normal to want to build your name or "build your kingdom," but in the kingdom of God, there are many rooms. Jesus has gone ahead of us to prepare a place for us. It is your job to receive it. Receive your inheritance!

RUN TO GOD

I took a ship stability class at a maritime academy in Fort Lauderdale, Florida, and it was one of the hardest classes I had ever taken. We were constantly doing exercises and formulas to figure out the center of gravity (COG) of the ship. The COG is vital to keeping a ship upright and not capsizing in order to get the ship from point A to point B.

Jesus is basically saying, "You are here at point A, and I will get you to point B!" So, what are you worried about? The beauty of it is that Jesus says there is more. He says, "Whoever comes to me will never be hungry or thirsty again." You can't use it all up. Your cup will runneth over.

Jesus is telling us to stop worrying about what we don't have and start focusing on what we do have. And when we do that, our stinkin' thinkin' begins to change from glass half empty to glass half full. Then and only then will we have the revelation that God is getting ready to do a new thing inside us and fill up our glasses!

When we fall short, and we will, or when we fall off the wagon, we must recognize that Jesus is right there extending a hand to us. He will pull us out of the pit just as he pulled Peter up out of the water when he began to sink.

When we have disobeyed God or gone astray, our first instinct is to run. However, Jesus says run to me:

> Come to me all you who are weary and burdened and I will give you rest. (Matthew 11:28)

Don't run *from* God—run *to* God!

Joshua was never interested in perfection; he never claimed to have all the answers. He simply obeyed God and allowed God to lead him. By having God as your compass, why wouldn't a nation desire to follow you? Sure, he had scars. He had seen the devastating impact of slavery and torture. He was led into the wilderness by a trusted advisor, and he watched so many people die before finally being called to stand up and lead an entire nation into the Promised Land.

The fear inside of him could have crippled him. It could have stopped him in his tracks. God commissioned Joshua for a great work, but what if Joshua had refused to answer the call? Joshua could have turned around and said, "I can't," "I have been told I'm not good enough," or "I will never amount to anything." All the negative voices in his head could have come to light in that moment. Most likely, God's will would have come into fruition through someone else, but there is a huge chance we would have never heard Joshua's name.

What takes a person from good to great is their ability to harness fear and push through to their purpose. Once you allow yourself to take some scars and lose a few battles, you are ready to lead. I'm not saying that you need to be a failure, but I am telling you that it takes failure in order to succeed. Michael Jordan said, "I fail over and over again—that is why I succeed."

Your place of biggest impact could be right where you are! God has so much more in store for you, but what God views as big in the kingdom of God can appear as very small to the world. In other words, trust God, live your life, and lead others. Coming from a broken place, it can seem hard to picture yourself leading your own self—much less anyone else. God is so much bigger than your imagination. You can't see it, but God can. We must fight. We must keep stepping. We can't go from one to six, but we can go from one to two, from two to three, and so on.

Jesus walked this earth as a perfect man, but he was a perfect God. No one took his life; instead, he laid down his life for your sins and mine. When we understand that, we can begin to live life the way it was meant to be lived. Jesus never promised an easy life, but he did promise to be with us in the midst of our struggles.

You owe it to yourself. You owe it to your broken and battered spirit to place all the junk at the foot of the altar, pick up this battle plan, and fight. This life is so short, and time flies by so fast; you don't want to get to the end of this life and realize the horrifying truth that you have been carrying this weight like a backpack for so many years.

Are you seeing it yet? We are slowly slipping away from that ghostly silhouette we discussed in previous chapters and are able to see our dream, our purpose, radiating with brilliance. You carry scars. You carry pain and hurt, but now you know that through all of this, you are being equipped each and every day for God's glory.

The biggest problem with your situation stares back at you in the mirror, but the answer to your biggest problem also stares back at you in the mirror. We are not measured by our talents or doings but by *Imago Dei*—recognizing we are made in the *image of God*—and realizing that God is in control.

A couple of months ago, I was riding on my lawnmower and listening to music. I love the deep thoughts that come to you when you are cutting grass. It's kind of like shower time, right? Yeah. It's super spiritual. Unless I'm singing "Bad" by Michael Jackson, right? As I was riding on my lawnmower, a voice said, "Study the heart."

What? Study the heart?

That night, I found myself researching the human heart. I started learning about the four chambers of the heart: the right atrium, the left atrium, the right ventricle, and the left ventricle.

I started learning about the tricuspid and the aorta. It was all fascinating stuff, but as I was looking at my computer, I thought, *What am I doing? I am literally watching YouTube videos on how the human heart works.*

The voice said, "That's not it."

I kept searching, and then I clicked on a colorful 3-D image of the human heart. I thought, *What is that?*

Now you might be asking, "What on earth are you talking about here?"

This gets good. Just hang in there with me for a minute.

In the 3-D image, there was a yellow outline of the electrical wiring of the human heart. It is designed to carry electricity throughout the heart.

I was drawn to a particular part of the electrical system. The center of the diagram had several lines labeling different parts of the heart, and there was a small bundle of cardiac muscle fibers that conducted the electrical impulses that regulate the heartbeat. In other words, they play a major role in setting the pace of the human heart and setting the stage for life in our own bodies.

Right away, I knew I had something very special. I called a doctor from my church and said, "John, what do you know about the human heart?"

He chuckled a bit and said, "Well, I have performed a few operations, so I know a little bit. What do you need to know?"

I said, "Can you tell me about this particular bundle of fibers?"

He got excited and started telling me all about it. "This bundle of fibers takes the command from the AV node in the right atrium and sends it down to the ventricles and tells them to contract. Dustin, you are on to something here. I have never heard anyone talk about this before, but this bundle actually sets the pace of the human heart. It sets the balance or the coordination of the electrical impulses within the heart, and without it would result in death."

Now that I have your attention—and you're wondering why we are so focused on this particular bundle of fibers—do you want to know the name of this bundle? It's called the bundle of His or His bundle.

I'm not making this up. You can look it up yourself. It's like a calling card or God's fingerprint in our design. It's beautiful. Wilhelm His Jr. discovered it in the 1800s.

Is that a coincidence? I'll let you decide, but for me, it's more proof that points toward God's amazing plan. We are created beings. We are not some weird by-product of evolution. That stuff's a joke. You are not alone.

We were created in the Imago Dei—in the image of God.

Do me a favor and check your pulse for a minute. Just feel it, *boom boom … boom boom … boom boom*. Keep your hand there for a minute. That rhythm that you feel is life pulsing through your body. *Boom boom*. Keep your hand there. No matter your social status, no matter what baggage you carry, no matter how great life may be for you at this time, we all have this rhythm or fingerprint—and we all come together under one roof in need of a Savior.

How closely does that *boom boom* resemble *knock knock, knock knock*? Jesus says, "Behold, I stand at the door and knock." Who is going to open that door today? Will you receive God's inheritance?

REFLECTION

1. What is meant by "receive your inheritance"?

   _____

   _____

   _____

2. The biggest problem with your situation stares back at you in the mirror, but the answer to your biggest problem also stares back at you in the mirror. What does this statement mean?

   _____

   _____

   _____

3. Do you find it comforting to know that the sound of your heartbeat resembles life pulsing through your veins?

   _____

   _____

   _____

Chapter 7
Live Your Legacy

> Love the Lord your God with all your heart, with all your soul, and with all your strength. These words that I am giving you today are to be in your heart. Repeat them to your children. Talk about them when you sit in your house and when you walk along the road, when you lie down and when you get up.
>
> —*Deuteronomy 6:5–7*

Let's pause and do a little recap of how far we have come. When you first opened this book, you were skeptical of what exactly you were getting yourself into. It's okay. You can admit it. I'm a big boy. I can take it. In fact, I also get it. I totally understand how it feels to pick up this book and say, "What can this possibly do for me? How can I move forward with all these scars?"

As you turned the pages, I hope you heard the voice of someone who has been in your shoes. Maybe the circumstances were a bit different, but the pain was the same. I hope you took each key battle principle seriously and really gave it a shot. If you did, then you know without a shadow of a doubt that it works! It's not easy. It's not perfect, but it works. With these principles, you can begin the healing process and begin to move toward your purpose.

By recapping how far we have come, we can catch a little glimpse of how far God wants to take us:

1. Prepare: Start to identify the problem and begin the first phase.
2. Obtain Spies: Surround yourself with people who care for you.
3. Cross the Jordan: Eventually, you have to move.
4. Defeat the Enemy: Recognize it's Christ who fights for you.
5. Claim Your Inheritance: Take your scars and lead others.

The sixth key battle principle is to live your legacy. After Joshua's farewell address in chapter 23, we find him giving this charge to his people:

> Therefore, fear the Lord and worship him in sincerity and truth. Get rid of the gods your fathers worshiped beyond the Euphrates River and in Egypt, and worship the Lord. But if it doesn't please you to worship the Lord, choose for yourselves today: Which will you worship—the gods your fathers worshiped beyond the Euphrates River or the gods of the Amorites in whose land you are living? As for me and my family, we will worship the Lord. (Joshua 24:14–15)

We have to make a choice and then act on that choice. Maybe your choices have been less than great. I was doing jail ministry with some friends. We would go and share the Word of God as well as our testimonies every Tuesday night for more than two years. I saw a lot of progress, but we noticed that the inmates kept winding up back in jail. They kept coming back because they were comfortable in their emptiness. They were comfortable in their chaos. That was natural. In fact, for our whole lives, we are taught to see life a certain way. Right or wrong, we are taught by our experiences, and these experiences are different for everybody, depending on environment and culture.

All of the little things that we were taught and experienced—from childhood all the way to our adult lives—shaped our worldviews. The whole time, we think this is just how it is. It will never get better. I'm here to tell you that is a lie straight from the pit of hell.

God desires *life* for us. It's about so much more than just going through the motions of day-to-day life. We are called to live out our legacies. Those who merely wake up and blindly begin their days as though they have no real meaning or impact are missing it. They are missing the grand splendor of this life and just how great it is. We serve a *big* God—so why don't we live like it? Why don't we live as though God Almighty is our compass?

If you lived each and every day as if you truly believe this, what legacy do you think you could leave behind? Just think of the people who would be affected by having someone like that in their lives—someone connected to the most powerful being in all eternity. I'm getting chills just thinking about it. Your legacy can be great. Your story is motivation to push others toward life and purpose. Just think of how great it would be to watch someone who is broken go from death to life.

You can be the vessel that delivers Jesus into their brokenness. You can be the missing piece that brings their puzzle to life. This has been a very tough road to walk with you, but the strength you have portrayed throughout this book has been amazing. Living your legacy allows you to walk in confidence, knowing that you are here for a purpose. Living your legacy allows you the freedom from living for the approval of others. There may be a time when you bring your request to God and don't *feel* different. There may be a time when you take it to God and don't *see* immediate change. However, your miracle could be right on the other side of your flipped perspective. Choosing to believe God and allowing him to use this hurt, pain, and fear is the very thing that will set you free.

I absolutely love this quote from the movie *Paul, Apostle of Christ*:

> Imagine yourself looking out at the vast sea before you. You reach down, and you put a hand into the water, and you scoop it up toward you.

> Immediately, the water starts leaking through your fingers until the hand is empty. That water is a man's life. From birth to death, it is always slipping through our hands until it is gone. Along with all that you hold dear in this world. And yet the kingdom I speak of, that I live for, is like the rest of the water out in the sea. Man lives for that cup of water that slips through his fingers. But those that follow Jesus Christ live for that endless expanse of sea.

The depth of this quote is so vast. Paul really puts life into perspective here. We are here for such a short time, and then we are gone. I don't know about you, but I don't really want to spend the rest of my life crippled with fear.

The words that God spoke to Joshua can be heard echoing throughout eternity: "Be strong and courageous." These words still stand with as much authority today as when they were first spoken.

Through God's grace and mercy, we can be strong and courageous. We can let down our guard against people. It is okay to trust again. It's okay to laugh again. Live your life. Shoot for your dreams. Take them out of hiding. Write them down right next to these six key battle principles so that you can see them and have a road map to get you there. I am so happy that you chose to walk this journey with me, and I assure you that these are the very tools that I have personally used to overcome my scars.

I have dealt with addiction firsthand, seen the devastating effects of infidelity in a marriage, lost what I thought was my livelihood (my career), lost a daughter to Potter syndrome, lost a mother to drug addiction, and dealt with ongoing health issues. I'm here to tell you that God is good! I don't deserve this platform.

People ask me all the time, "How are you qualified to do this?"

I reply, "I'm not! I'm equipped. God has equipped me for his purpose, which is his glory."

Through the process and through the scars, I can effectively apply these battle principles in my life to lay the groundwork for God to use my tragedy and turn it into triumph. Without the hardships, I would not be the man I am today. Without the scars, there is no way I could confidently lead others to find their purpose. Applying these principles to my life was a six-step process to victory. I can now live my life as though I am a child of God. I am dead to sin and raised to new life.

Doesn't that sound great? Maybe you aren't fully there yet, but trust in the process. God is doing great work inside you. There may be parts of principles that you will use for the rest of your life, such as counseling, obtaining the right people in your life who look out for your best interests, and relying on Christ to fight for you. That's the beauty of it. This system will continue to help you fight for the rest of your life—and you thought you were just buying another book!

When you are living your legacy, people will be drawn to you, they will be willing to listen, and you will have great influence on their lives. I don't want to be around people who are haphazardly stumbling through life. I want to be beside people who are living out their legacies.

No matter what stage of life you find yourself in, it's not too late. It is never too late to turn to God and allow him to guide your steps. Even if you find yourself reading this book in the hardest of prisons, there are people in prison who are freer than others will ever be. Even if you find yourself advanced in age, remember God's words to Joshua:

> You have become old, advanced in age, but a great deal of the land remains to be possessed. (Joshua 13:1)

There is a great work to do. Get up and go! You can no longer worry about the chains that kept you from pursuing your dream. You can no longer worry about the slavery to addiction, the slavery to depression, or the chains attaching you to pornography. It is time to be free. It is time to *live*.

Living with hope means having faith—even during the storm. The size of your storm shows your importance to the kingdom. The devil knows exactly who you are. He knows exactly what you are capable of; he wouldn't even bother with you if you weren't valuable.

When life feels completely chaotic and confusion is around every corner, don't look to the left or to the right. Look *up*. Look up to your heavenly Father. He created you with his perfect hands and has given your life purpose.

> This book of instruction must not depart from your mouth; you are to meditate on it day and night so that you may carefully observe everything written in it. For then you will prosper and succeed in whatever you do. (Joshua 1:8)

To stand firm through the storm, we must stay rooted in the Word of God. This life calls for faith.

Joshua wasn't just born knowing how to be a leader. He didn't just pop out of the womb as this valiant warrior. No, it took a process. All his trials and experiences made him who he was. Joshua's obedience to God allowed him to lead a nation. He faced tragedy, pressure, fear, and hurts, but he never lost sight of his Compass. He allowed faith in God and the Word of God to lead him every step of the way. Even though he lost some battles, he still won and led the entire nation to fulfill their purpose and inherit what was rightfully theirs.

The six key battle principles:

1. Prepare
2. Obtain Spies
3. Cross the Jordan
4. Defeat the Enemy
5. Claim Your Inheritance
6. Live Your Legacy

REFLECTION

1. What does it look like for you to live your personal legacy?

   _____
   _____
   _____

2. What do I mean when I say, "There are people in prison who are freer than others will ever be"? How can someone be free and locked up at the same time?

   _____
   _____
   _____

3. How are you going to use your scars to help someone else?

   _____
   _____
   _____

My Prayer for You

I really hope you have enjoyed taking this journey with me. My biggest hope is that you received a blessing as you read this book. My desire is to lay the groundwork for you to be able to move past your scars and begin the healing process. With the six key battle principles, I believe you can start to heal, and I also believe they will give you a road map to life.

There is freedom to be found through the love and grace of our Lord Jesus Christ. As I write these words, I am praying for you. I want you to be sure that you are not alone. The battle you are facing is a very big deal, but it is very small compared to the power of God.

I am praying that you grasp the totality of who you are in Christ. There is nothing that you have done or gone through that can separate you from the love of Christ. Believe in yourself! You can move forward. You may never forget, but you can forgive. You can move forward from this and use it as a testament to others for how great God is.

If you haven't taken that first step toward accepting Christ into your heart as your Lord and Savior, let's start today. Let's do it together. Repeat these words after me:

> Jesus, I'm a sinner in need of your grace. I come to you today in total surrender of my own fleshly desires. I'm asking you to come into my heart as my Lord and Savior. It is my desire to follow

you for the rest of my life. I believe that you died
on that cruel, rugged cross, and three days later,
you rose again with our freedom in your hands.
I repent of my sin and give my life to you.

Congratulations! The Bible tells us that if you believe in your heart that Jesus is Lord and repent of your sin, you will be saved. If you prayed this prayer with me today and meant it in your heart, we will spend eternity together in a place called heaven with Jesus Christ our Lord.

You can rejoice in the fact that, at the end of the day, through all of the hardship and the difficulty, through the pain and hurt, God is still on the throne. He is for you, and if He is for you, then *nothing* can ever stand against you.

Please don't misunderstand me, I am not saying that everything will be easy now, but you can rest easy knowing the God of the universe is walking with you.

Let's pray:

Father, I come to you in bold expectation that the words in this book will bring much life. I pray for wisdom and freedom from the bondage that has entangled me. Allow me to grow and heal under your mercy. Help me, Father, to move from broken to whole. I need you to direct and guide me in your ways, God. As I come against trials and hurts, I know that you are with me and that I can use the principles in this book to help move me forward. Thank you, God, for showing me what love looks like. Help me take my tragedy and turn it into triumph.